6 Steps to Tapping Into Your Creative Genius:

How to Manifest Your Dreams Using Intuition, Creativity, and Meditation

by Alise Spiritual Healing & Wellness Center

All Rights Reserved. No parts of this book may be used or reproduced by any means, graphic, electronic, or mechanical, including photocopying, recording, taping or by any information storage retrieval system without the written permission of the author except in the case of brief quotations embodied in critical articles and reviews.

This book may be ordered through booksellers or by contacting:

iGlobal Educational Services, LLC
PO Box 94224 Phoenix, AZ 85070
www.iglobaleducation.com
512-761-5898

Because of the dynamic nature of the Internet, any web addresses or links contained in this book may have changed since publication and may no longer be valid. The views expressed in this work are solely those of the author and do not necessarily reflect the views of the publisher, and the publisher hereby disclaims any responsibility for them.

6 Steps to Tapping Into Your Creative Genius: *How to Manifest Your Dreams Using Intuition, Creativity, and Meditation*

Copyright © 2018 Alise Spiritual Healing & Wellness Center and Dr. Alicia Holland

ISBN-13: 978-1-944346-81-2

DEDICATION

This book is dedicated to all individuals who are looking or have already tapped into their Creative Genius. Your spiritual gifts and talents will make room for you in this World so it is your divine birthright to get to know your born identity. Know that you are not alone and that you are loved, you are valued, and you are competent. It's time to unleash your Creative Genius!

ASSUMPTIONS

In order to provide you with material to meet your unique spiritual needs, we had to make some basic assumptions. We assume the following:

1. You understand the Spirit, God, Great Divine, is also called a higher power.
2. You understand that your higher self is your real self or born identity.
3. You want information on how to tap into your creative genius to manifest your dreams using intuition, creativity, and meditation.
4. You have a desire to connect to your intuition through your chosen spiritual practice.

ACKNOWLEDGMENTS

I cannot say this enough, but I must give glory to God for helping me realize my potential and purpose in life. It was He whom brought Charlotte and Alexa-Rae together to manifest this project. There are truly no words to express my gratitude as each of you are truly a blessing to our healing center.

I also want to thank Surendra for his creativity in formatting, Dondee for his creativity in designing our book. Each of you are amazing!

TABLE OF CONTENTS

STEP 1: Develop a Spiritual Practice 9

STEP 2: Journal Your Way to Spiritual Cleansing
　　　　and Negativity 26

STEP 3: Connect With Nature and Its Cousins 40

STEP 4: Sustaining A Meditation Practice 51

STEP 5: Practice Mindfulness and Track It 57

STEP 6: Get to Know Your Angels By Name 63

Class Tours and Conferences 71

Notes 72

STEP 1:
Develop a Spiritual Practice

We exist in a world with two distinctly opposite divisions.

There is both a material and a non-material world.

Though the material world is extremely important, as it is the part of our existence in which we can take physical action, it is a mere result of the non-material world.

Unfortunately, education at large focuses mainly on the material world.

We are not formally taught how to love, how to deal with emotions, how to love ourselves, how to be confident, how beliefs shape our reality, how to find out what you really believe, how to find and sustain happiness, how to find fulfillment, how to deal with difficult situations and most importantly, how to find our true selves.

Instead we are taught how to calculate the square root of pi, the importance of supply and demand, and how to drive a car.

Don't get me wrong, all this information is invaluable, but it should not be at the expense of understanding the true nature of reality and understanding ourselves.

As a result of our neglect of the non-material world, with all the knowledge we have of the material world, there is still an increasing number of unfulfilled, unhappy, humans.

If we were to see the importance of understanding the non-material world in the same light, then perhaps we would have more balanced humans who are equally materially, emotionally and spiritually successful.

Spiritual practices offer us a way back to ourselves.

It generously affords us the opportunity of learning about the most important things in life on our own.

The problem however is that since spiritual practices are not widely celebrated or promoted, most people are uninformed on the topics. Most people feel that something is missing and wish to turn to spiritual practices, but they don't know where to start and how to begin.

If you're one of these people, keep reading, we'll give you some ideas.

What is a Spiritual Practice?

At the heart of it, a spiritual practice refers to any activity which is actively and continuously repeated, not for perfection, but in an effort to bring us closer to the truth of who we really are.

It presents us with the highly esteemed opportunity to consciously evolve and grow with nature.

Spiritual practices help us get a better grip on who we really are without the chaos of life.

They offer us a chance to unplug from the material world and go deeper into ourselves.

It helps us to understand both who we are on the material plane and the non-material plane.

Due to intense focus on the material world, people rarely have the opportunity to find out who they really are. A lot of people are living inside the body of stranger. They unconsciously try to fit in with the external world that they have completely neglected their own beliefs and interests. We conform to the idea that material things make us happy, or that having a formal education in something sustainable is what we really want. However, often when people really start to inquire within, they realize that they have completely different goals and ideals.

In addition to giving us the ability to better explore our external identity, spiritual practices give us insight into our non-material identify. Who we really are goes far beyond our material identity.

Spiritual activity makes us feel connected to a power higher than ourselves.

With all that being said, spiritual activity is not confined to yoga, meditation or prayer.

Spiritual activity shape shifts into a myriad of forms such as painting, journaling, hiking, swimming, dancing, writing and the list goes on and one.

Once we begin to feel closer to ourselves and connected to a higher power, we are practicing some form of spiritual activity. If you don't know where to begin, that's okay. Let's take look at a few daily spiritual practices that you can try, which include the following:

| Prayer | Meditation | Yoga | Tai Chi |

Prayer

Prayer is perhaps the most popular and widespread spiritual practice. Prayer involves entering a dialogue with whomever or whatever entity you consider to be the greater power which in responsible for and in control of existence as we know it. It is our own personal one-way line to the divine. In other words, you are the one talking to the Spirit.

Prayer is an extremely useful daily spiritual practice. It requires no effort, it is personal, and it is a direct line to a higher power. All you need to do is close your eyes and talk.

Talk about what you're feeling, talk about what you want to accomplish, talk about your fears, talk about what you are grateful for, talk about what you need to know, talk about your problems, talk about anything.

It doesn't matter whether or not there is someone really listening, what matters is how you feel about praying and how you feel about who or what you're talking to. Sometimes just letting it out is good enough.

Often times, we find the answers and the growth we need by verbally letting out whatever is on our minds. Daily prayer can and if practiced will help you on your never-ending journey of personal development.

It is important to note that prayer is your way of letting the Spirit know what you desire and what is going on. However, it is equally important to be in Meditation as well.

Try This...

Developing Your Personal Prayer Strategy

- Take some time out of your day to really think about your prayer life.
- Spend some time thinking about how your prayer life can be improved?
- Develop a plan and accountability to improve it.
- Pray around your school campus early one morning each week with another leader or two

Self-Reflection: Connecting with God/Spirit/ Great Divine/Higher Power through Prayer

1. What is your definition of prayer?

   _____
   _____
   _____
   _____
   _____

2. How can your prayer life be improved?

   _____
   _____
   _____
   _____
   _____

3. Do you have a personal space for your spiritual practice? Why or why not?

   _____
   _____
   _____
   _____
   _____

4. How can prayer partners enhance your prayer life?

   _____
   _____
   _____
   _____

Meditation and Mindfulness

Meditation is the scientific art form of detaching from unnecessary and compulsive thought to be truly present and appreciate what is happening now.

Our minds are usually focused on the past or the future; it is rare that we are truly present and appreciating everything life has to offer. Meditation affords us a route to escape the dreadful affliction of unorganized and compulsive thought so that we can find our way back to our true selves and to a higher source.

There are several types of meditation, mindfulness, Zen, Tibetan, and so etcetera, but at the heart of it, they all share the same goal—enlightenment.

We, the human beings, have a tendency to be more in the repair mode than in the prevention stage, at least most of the time. We often tend to take liberties with our mental and physical selves, disregarding the potential consequences of our actions.

Self-Reflection: Questions to Ponder

1. How often is it that you recognize the symptoms of stress and fatigue, which your mind and body emit so frequently?

   _____
   _____
   _____
   _____
   _____

2. Do you ever slow down and let your senses repair? Why or why not?

_____
_____
_____
_____
_____

As human beings, we just forge ahead in our worldly pursuits. It is for this reason that the ancient art of meditation has the most relevance for the busy and stressed out man of today. Within meditation, it is mindfulness which takes the center stage, since it helps you focus on a single point in your mind.

There are so many different types of meditation and mindfulness strategies, so you can easily try to find the one that will benefit you on a daily basis.

Let's take a look at some types of meditations which you can introduce into your daily life:

Walking Meditation	Sitting Meditation	Prayer Meditation

Walking Meditation

Walking meditation, as its name says, uses the walking experience as a way to focus. You observe your surroundings while walking, taking in everything in your environment, keeping your awareness level high.

Take a deep breath, then start walking at a normal pace. As you walk, feel the air flow, hear the sounds of nature, or the sounds of a bustling city, depending on where you are. Feel the earth under your feet, and with each step, feel the difference your movement makes in the environment. Take everything in. As you move, you will become increasingly aware of your own body, and experiencing the outside world will help you get in touch with your inner self.

It is common knowledge that walking is very beneficial for your health. By practicing the walking meditation, not only do you improve your health, but you walk a spiritual path, too.

If you're not comfortable enough with the city traffic, try searching for a park, or an oasis in nature for your first attempts at the walking meditation.

Sitting Meditation

The most commonly known kind of meditation is the sitting meditation. You settle in a comfortable position, keeping your spine straight, your chin pulled back, and your lower body comfortable as you let the energy flow through your chakras.

It's important to stay comfortable, as meditating in a sitting position can prove challenging for the inexperienced. Be mindful of the factors that may make this kind of meditation difficult, such as the room temperature, having your stomach full, outside noise and other distractions.

Take deep, slow breaths. With each breath, you form a connection to the Spirit. With your lower chakras, you become deeply rooted, while the upper allow you to reach out to the Heavens, to the Universe. Becoming one with the world, you enrich your humanity with the Divine.

Sitting meditation is healthy for the spirit, because it provides uninterrupted energy flow down your spine, which moves to the other sections of your body, healing you, while your mind reaches for the full awareness.

It can be a humbling, deeply moving experience.

Prayer Meditation

Prayer meditation is a form of reflecting upon the revelations directed from the Spirit, where you became aware of His intentions for you. You retain your focus on a specific thought, a question, or a religious passage, and reflect on it, keeping the Universal nature of the Spirit's love in mind.

By practicing the prayer meditation, the personal relationship between you and the Spirit springs and grows into a beautiful tree, connecting you to the Divine. This tree is as healthy as your thoughts are clear, with your faith like water, giving it life, and your hope like the Sun, keeping it strong.

Prayer meditation is more structured and concise than a regular prayer, and though it serves a similar purpose, it provides a stronger link to the Spirit by searching for the answers from inside you.

As you meditate, you allow the Spirit to enter your soul, providing a better understanding of the theme of your prayer as you ponder its message.

These are just three types of meditations that can help you throughout your daily life.

As you are using these meditations, it is extremely important to journal your experiences and reflect upon them. If you are not able to do this on a daily basis, then just jot down the biggest 'aha' moments so that you can begin to see a pattern of any changes in your thought patterns, behaviors, and choices. Most importantly, you should document your ability to focus and be mindful of our choices.

Keeping Your Meditation and Mindfulness Journal: What You Need to Include In It

A journal is your best friend when you are trying to practice meditation and just grow in all areas of your life. If you do not feel comfortable writing in a journal, then you can record an audio post about your meditation experiences or record a video.

Whatever you decide to do, you need to make sure that you include some key information.

Self-Reflection: Connecting with Your Meditations

1. What insights did you have as you meditated? Please be specific and feel free to summarize your insights for one day or multiple days to see a pattern.

   _____
   _____
   _____
   _____
   _____
   _____
   _____
   _____
   _____
   _____
   _____
   _____
   _____
   _____
   _____

_____
_____
_____
_____
_____
_____
_____
_____
_____
_____

Here's how you can introduce meditation into your daily life, with a special focus on mindfulness, and let it enrich your existence.

Mindfulness

Do we really know what meditation and mindfulness are all about, and how exactly each of these can help us when used alongside creativity?

When you meditate, you basically learn to focus on the core of your existence and get in touch with your inner self. The main benefits of meditation are relaxation and improvement in concentration, which allows you to connect to both your intuition and creativity.

Mindfulness takes you a step further and helps you focus on the epicenter of your thought process, whether it involves a situation, a problem, or an individual. It helps you divert all your energies towards the present moment, so that you can pay attention to a single aspect in your life. Eventually, you end up in a state of mind where you can simply focus on the issue or thought at hand, without allowing any other feeling to disturb your concentration.

Once you've understood how useful meditation and mindfulness are to you, you then need to look into what the best course of action for your situation is. To begin, it is important that you start using the core breathing exercises, as a part of whole-body meditation.

With help from your spiritual guru, learn to focus on your breathing patterns. This will help you regain your composure, and it will give you some relief from stress.

Why It Works

So, what is it that makes meditation and mindfulness work? Since the human mind is full of conflicting thoughts and emotions, it is often very difficult to focus and stay calm. Such practices help you regain your focus in life and concentrate on the present moment, teaching you how to react to distractions around you.

Meditation basically makes the brain waves move from a higher to lower frequency, which brings you closer to inner peace. As your thoughts become slower, you'll find it easier to process them, and to look at things from a different angle. This new perspective helps you reach the state of awareness necessary to connect with the nature of the world, as it is intended for you as a spiritual being.

The modern life is fast, too fast for the gentle nature of our souls. As we are forced to deal with the difficulties in our daily lives, meditation and mindfulness help us slow down and explore our problems with the newly found information from the other side of the spectrum of human life.

Now, let's go through two more powerful spiritual practices—Yoga and Tai Chi—that will help you connect with your intuition to tap into your own creative genius.

Yoga

Born in India, Yoga is a spiritual practice which is directed at connecting the mind, body and spirit. Yoga focuses on using meditation, breathing techniques and posture control to allow the mind, body and spirit to function as one ridiculously well-oiled machine.

There are several different types of yoga that focus on different aspects of the techniques and use different methodologies to complete the same task.

For example, Kundalini yoga focuses more of the meditative and physiological aspects of the mind and body to connect us to a power much greater than ourselves while balancing out the unison in which our mind, body and soul works.

Meanwhile, Ashtanga yoga focuses more on breathing techniques and posture manipulation to produce a large amount of physical activity and thereby sweat, which purifies and detoxifies our bodies, thereby helping to bring the three components in harmony.

There exist many different styles of yoga, and we are certain that one variation will speak to you. This is where the benefit of connecting to your intuition will help you know when it is time to begin this type of spiritual practice. If you find a daily yoga practice and you undertake each session with the intention to merge your mind, body and spirit to increase your wholeness as an individual, we guarantee that you will not be disappointed with how grounded and at peace you will feel each day.

Tai Chi

Though Yoga and Tai Chi are two separate disciplines, they share the common focus of uniting the mind, body and spirit. Tai Chi is sometimes described as meditation in motion.

It is a complex art form which combines the tranquility and focus of meditation with the grace and discipline of smooth continuous movements.

The main difference physical difference between Tai Chi and Yoga is that your body is in continuous but gentle motion. Much like Yoga, there are different versions of Tai Chi.

There's bound to be one version of this Chinese Spiritual Practice that resonates with your need of finding yourself and connecting with a higher power.

In addition to its spiritual benefits, Tai Chi has a wide range of physical benefits such as anxiety and stress relief. All in all, this is a great spiritual practice to employ if your intuition leads you down this route to help tap into your creative genius.

Now, you may be asking yourself the following question:

How long does it take to develop a daily spiritual practice?

The answer to this question really depends on you and your ability to be willing, ready, and able to commit to connecting to your higher self and accessing divine intelligence through your intuition.

As a general rule of thumb, it takes 30 days to form any habit. In the case, you will need to allow yourself at least 30 days to develop a daily spiritual practice.

Here are a few tips that can help you with your daily spiritual practice:

Seven Tips to Help with Implementing Your Daily Spiritual Practice

1. Create a schedule.
2. Do your spiritual practice the same time every day.
3. Do not judge yourself for not sticking to the schedule.
4. Focus on returning to the schedule, if you miss 1 or more days.
5. If you feel resistance, keep going, sticking to the practice will become easier over time.
6. Develop a spiritual practice that you enjoy. Ask Your Intuition for Guidance.
7. Be present; do not reduce the practice to a means to an end.

Finding an Area for Your Spiritual Practice

A sacred altar is a space wholly dedicated to a spiritual practice. It could be the place which you go to seek refuge and connect with yourself and a higher power, or the place you go to meditate or undertake whatever spiritual practices you might undertake.

Selecting a space in your home sends a signal to yourself and others that your spiritual practices are a very important aspect in your life. The space is usually adorned with spiritual ornaments such as Angels, Sacred Statues, Objects which are of sentimental value to you or things that make you feel most like yourself. Additionally, your sacred altar could include decorations from nature such as flowers or plants, anything that connects you to yourself and a higher power.

Self-Reflection: What's in Your Sacred Altar?

1. What do you plan on including in your Sacred Altar?
   _____
   _____
   _____
   _____
   _____

2. In what area of your living space would make a great location to pray, meditate, and/or reflect?
   _____
   _____
   _____
   _____
   _____

3. Why did you select this particular area of your living space for your Sacred Altar?
   _____
   _____
   _____
   _____
   _____

4. How do you plan on incorporating journal writing and creativity into your sacred altar?
   _____
   _____
   _____
   _____
   _____

The bottom line is that you must have a spiritual practice in place so that you can connect to your intuition to allow your creative side to come through in your daily activities. Now that you have learned the step on how to develop a spiritual practice, it's time to focus on the second step in how to tap into your creative genius.

STEP 2:
Journal Your Way to Spiritual Cleansing and Negativity

Journaling cannot merely be described a healthy habit; it is ultimately a spiritual cleansing. There is just something so very special about giving life to your thoughts through shaping them into words. Often times, journaling can also be used to keep track of spiritual visions, intuitive insights, dreams, goals, and whatever strikes your fancy.

It would serve each and every one of us to take some time to journal our thoughts and feelings down. There is tremendous potential for both personal and spiritual development just through the simple act of writing things down.

Five Benefits of Journaling

There are five benefits of journaling that should be taking note of which include the following:

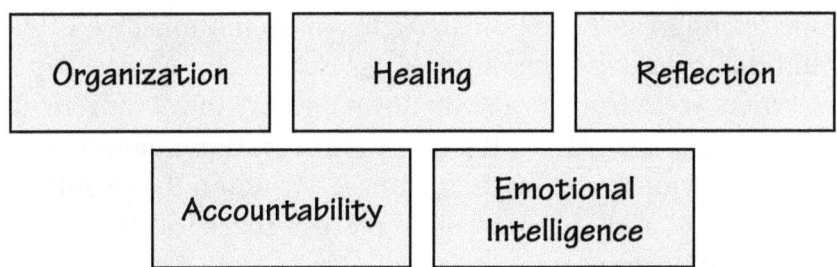

Organization

The first benefit of journaling is organization. Journaling helps us to organize our thoughts and clear our head space. Often when we don't know what to do about a situation, or when our heads are clouded with a variety of thought, journaling affords us the opportunity to pen everything down.

In penning down our thoughts and feelings we get to really sort them out and put them in their places to come to a conclusion, or just to feel better to have gotten everything off our chest.

It can literally feel like a weight has dropped off your shoulders as you move your thoughts from out your head, through your fingers and on to a page. The goal is to get the ideas out of your head and on paper, so it is okay if you write them down and away for a few hours or even a few days. The ideas are there so you will need to make sure that you keep it in a safe place to return to your thoughts. The bottom line is that you will be able to better analyze your thought process and come to solid conclusions that will help guide you on your lifelong quest to both spiritual and personal growth.

Healing

Going hand in hand with organization is the second benefit of journaling—healing. Through the recording and organizing of our deepest thoughts and emotions, we often find the formula for healing.

When we're forced to write down and organize, we start to put the pieces together. We start to process these emotions as a method emerges from the madness. We admit the problems to ourselves, and our awareness creates a space for the resolution to be born.

There may be times when you do not want to share with others what you are going through at that moment. You may not be ready to talk about it, but you can write about it in your journal to get it out of your system. Sometimes, our stories need to be told and a journal is a good way to write it down knowing that you have released it to the Universe.

Self-Reflection: Using Your Journal for Healing

1. How have your used a journal for recording your deepest thoughts and emotions to help you heal from situations in your life? If you never have done so, think about a situation that you are going through right now and write it down in your journal.

   _____
   _____
   _____
   _____

2. How did you feel after you wrote down your deepest thoughts and emotions for healing in your journal?

   _____
   _____
   _____
   _____

Reflection

The third benefit of journaling is reflection. Journaling provides us with an opportunity to take a good look at how we have developed over a period of time. Through recording our thoughts, emotions, problems and the resolutions to these problems, we begin to paint a picture of who we are and who we have grown to be.

We can use our past problems and scenarios to develop insight into problems that tend to reoccur. We have documented proof of our transgressions and we can begin to reflect and see where improvement needs to take place, and applaud ourselves for progress that has been made.

In addition to reflection, journals are also used for documenting improvement on things done over the years. It is a good way to estimate the events of one's life. We begin to relive our dearest memories each time we revisit our journal. Journaling almost quite literally affords us the unfathomable gift of time travel, whereby we revisit the events of the past.

Self-Reflection: Using Your Journal for Reflecting on Improvement

1. How have your used a journal for reflecting on your goals towards improving one or more areas of your life?

   _____
   _____
   _____
   _____
   _____

2. If you never have done so, think about a situation that you are going through right now and write it down in your journal. What was your biggest take-a-way from this situation? What did you learn about yourself?

_____
_____
_____
_____
_____

Accountability

Journals hold you accountable. Writing down your thoughts, emotions, problems, resolutions, and goals are a good way to keep yourself accountable. Physically reading about your struggles and plans is a good source of motivation for solving your problems and sticking to your plans.

Writing has this permanent feel to it; it is as if anything you have written somehow leaves your mind and becomes immortal through your words. Scientifically speaking, one is more inclined to honor a goal if it is written down somewhere. You have a physical means to keep track of your goals and the steps you have taken to accomplish them.

Physical reminders in the form of words often serve as catalysts to efficient personal growth. Documenting our progress motivates us to make more progress to document to keep the chemicals release from the feelings of being proud and happy circulating in our brains.

Increased Emotional Intelligence

By continuously writing down our thoughts and emotions, we become increasingly competent in dealing with them.

Through penning down the exact details of our experiences, we create a means for organization of these events which provide us with an opportunity to dive deeper and analyze our behavioral patterns. We begin to identify patterns, identify triggers and we know what to do to fix them. We become greater processors of emotions, which in turns gives us greater control over our lives.

Try This...

1. Document Your Feelings each day for one week. What did you learn about yourself?

   _____
   _____
   _____
   _____

TIP: If you wish, you can try this for an additional week or at least 30-days to see how this works. The more often you do this, the more you will be able to analyze your behavioral patterns, triggers, and work on ways to fix them.

Now that we have explored the benefits of keeping a journal, let's delve into the subject matter of the things one can write about.

Keeping a journal is useful for recording things such as thoughts, emotions, dreams, visions, life situations, problems, things to reflect on, resolutions, goals and the list goes on and on.

Thoughts

The documentation of thought is great for organizing and processing different thoughts. You may be uncertain about what you think about a person with whom you are beginning to have a relationship. Writing down the various thoughts presents a way for us to create a form of pros and cons list which will better inform us about what decision we should make about this person.

Dreams and Visions

Documenting dreams is a great way to gain some insight as to what is occurring inside our subconscious minds. Dreams often tell us what is bothering us deep down inside, or giving us insight as to what we really believe. In addition to this, we usually lose the memory of our dreams a few minutes after we rejoin waking life. Journaling as soon as we wake up will help us to immortalize the important points of our dreams for analysis.

Connecting with our subconscious is essentially connecting with our true selves. Often we don't really know what kind of beliefs have been forced fed to us through media, society and even our friends and families. Recording our dreams through journaling and then analyzing them is a good way to dive deep down into our subconscious minds in an effort to see what's really stored in there.

Emotions

Documenting our emotions are useful for the processing of emotions. The manipulation of emotions is always a tricky topic. We often make impulsive decisions based on the overwhelming control of our dominant emotions. Writing them down allows us to work them out before we make hasty decisions. Through writing we organize these emotions and take some time to work them out and put some logic behind them so that we can make more informed decisions as we take action in our daily lives.

The time you dedicate to journaling is completely dependent on you and your motivation to journal. It depends also on your need for journaling and the benefits which you will personally derive.

Daily journaling is however theoretically beneficial for everyone. It gifts us the opportunity of keeping track of our mental processes for reflection aimed at improvement and for praise aimed at progress.

Setting aside at least 15 minutes each day to journal is a healthy habit which will lead to immense growth in the area of emotional intelligence as well as tremendous spiritual growth.

If you're going to be journaling, especially every day, you need to find ways to ensure that your journal is safe from prying eyes. After all, having a journal is a completely personal endeavor. Though we cannot guarantee that your journal will be 100% safe, we can give you some advice on the best ways to keep it secure.

Tips on Keeping Your Journal Private
Disclaimer

The first tip is to write a disclaimer on the front page of your diary. Play on the guilt of the future reader. Let them know how personal and important the words on these pages are to you and what a huge violation of your privacy it would be if they read your personal thoughts and emotions.

This isn't the safest option, but it is bound to guilt trip a few people and deter them from digging through your journal.

Safe Hiding Places

The second tip is to find a safe hiding place. This might be very extreme, but you can keep your diary in safe places such as safes where only you know the combination. Another alternative to a safe is to get a diary that comes with a combination lock. These are fairly safe; most people wouldn't want you to know that they've read your journal, so they wouldn't be very excited about having to literally break the lock off your book to get a piece of your writing. In addition to a safe, you could hide your journal in places where people are unlikely to visit, such as a secret compartment in your floorboards, walls or ceilings.

Keep a Digital Journal

The third tip is to keep a digital journal. Though this may feel less personal and connected than a traditional book and pen journal, a digital journal is a good way to keep your thoughts safe as you have the option to protect it via a password. Freeware programs like MacJournal are good resources you can use to start a digital journal. Day One & Journey are fantastic modern journaling apps! Digital journals are also beneficial because often they can be accessed by all your devices; your laptop, smartphone, or even a friend's computer. This means that you can journal wherever you are if the need arises. You won't need to worry about forgetting your book and waiting until you reach home to write down your thoughts, or sleeping over somewhere and not having your journal to write your dream down.

Connecting To Your Higher Self

There are two aspects of the self. When I say the word self what I mean is who you are, i.e., there are two aspects to who you are.

For argument's sake we'll call the two aspects the lower self and the higher self.

The lower self can be related to your conscious mind. Your lower self deals with your physical self or your physical identity. How you think, what you say, what you do, your likes, your dislikes, your attributes, in essence, your built personality.

The higher self can be related to your subconscious mind. It refers to a God like aspect of ourselves. It refers to the intuitive part of ourselves that sometimes just knows things. It refers to the creative part of ourselves through which life seems to act through. Most creative types such as writers, filmmakers, artists, dancers, painters, actors, and etcetera know that we create from a part of ourselves which is bigger than us. Your higher self is your direct connection to something greater than yourself.

Your higher self is the part of you which has known everything and continues to know everything about how life really works. The problem is that we have become so disconnected from our higher self that it is almost completely obscured by our lower selves. You know when you have accessed your higher self when certain universal truths seem to resonate on a deeply inexplicable level. You begin to uncover all the truths that are embedded deep down in our true beings.

The fastest and most efficient way to access our higher selves are through spiritual practices. Spiritual practices grant us a pathway to finding both ourselves and our spiritual guides. Spiritual practices focus the mind and allow us to discard what is false and center our being on our real nature and all that is true.

Practices such as meditation, yoga and prayer are direct routes which take us back to our true selves; our higher selves. Through these routes we bypass our lower selves and utilize our one-way ticket to our ultimate truths. These powerful spiritual practices clear our minds and sharpens our intuition.

The key to accessing our higher selves lies in quieting our mind; decreasing unnecessary mental chatter. The mental chatter of the mind promotes our separation from our true selves. Once the mind is quiet, we find the key to experiencing our true nature. With a quiet mind we filter out the unnecessary and compulsive mental chatter which isolates us from the truth, the truth about who we are and the truth that can be found by accessing our spiritual helpers.

Guardian angels are celestial energetic beings which have been prescribed to us from birth to help us to navigate through life. Spirit guides however are beings which were once people living and breathing just like you here on Earth. They have fulfilled their Earthly destinies and have been promoted to the position of spirit guide. They've also been entrusted with the task of seeing you successfully through your life. They are our own personal helpers through every aspect of our personal growth.

As elusive as these characters may seem, it is possible to connect to them. We can get direct answers and guidance through our problems in life. Through the following of the following pathways we can directly access our spiritual guides and archangels.

Meditation as mentioned before is a great way. By meditation you quiet your mind and clear yourself of negative energy which brings down your vibration. By elevating your vibration, you get closer and closer to the vibration of your spirit guides which increases your chances of being able to reach them.

Having a healthy diet and partaking in an exercise routine serves to raise the vibration of your body to match the vibration of your mind to facilitate a mind-body machine. Your body literally creates you who are. "You are what you eat"; remember? When your body is functioning optimally, it means your organs which are needed for perception are also functioning normally. This means you'll be able to detect the presence of your spirit guides more easily. Your hearing, sense of sight, virtually all your senses as well as your intuition will be heightened.

Raising your overall vibration will take you closer to your guides. Our spiritual guides and archangels exist in a realm that we can't readily perceive. Everything in life is measured in terms of energy and vibration. In raising our own energy levels and therefore vibrational frequencies, we become closer to the realm that our spiritual guides and archangels exist in. Our vibration can be raised by the practice of sustaining the feeling of happiness and love. Focusing on positive thoughts and experience will take us closer to where we need to be.

Call upon your archangel, the Holy Spirit or any angel within the angelic realm. Calling upon them is good way to reach out to them. When you actively call out to them, you're setting your intentions and opening in up your energy towards them. Opening up our intention to communicating with our spiritual guides and archangels allows us to be more attentive to receiving their signals; our intuition is heightened as we earnestly await their presence.

When you call upon them in earnest, they will heed your cry. All you need to do is pay attention and acknowledge their presence. You will be sure to get signs of their presence. Listen out for feelings in the body, or something drawing your attention to a particular book, imagery or otherwise.

Your intuition will play a huge role on your quest to reach out to your higher self and your spirit guides and other residents of the seemingly untouchable realm. Pay attention to things you may feel. Your mind-body instrument is a well-oiled machine. Physical symptoms usually have some counterpart in our mind, whether we can decipher it or not. You may feel called to go to a certain place, stop a certain activity or undertake a new one. Listen to your gut feeling, it often knows more than you do.

There are also a wide array of prayers which one can utilize to quiet one's mind in order to be closer to the supernatural realm of guides and archangels.

Below are some bible verses that can help you as you begin to meditate:

Bible Verses To Help During Meditation

Philippians 3:13-14 No, dear brothers and sisters, I have not achieved it, but I focus on this one thing: Forgetting the past and looking forward to what lies ahead.

Colossians 3:1 Therefore, if you have been raised with the Messiah, keep focusing on the things that are above, where the Messiah is seated at the right hand of God.

Philippians 3:13-14 No, dear brothers and sisters, I have not achieved it, but I focus on this one thing: Forgetting the past and looking forward to what lies ahead.

Colossians 3:2 - Set your affection on things above, not on things on the earth.
Philippians 4:13 - I can do all things through Christ which strengthened me.
Proverbs 16:3 - Commit thy works unto the LORD, and thy thoughts shall be established.
Proverbs 3:5-6- Trust in the LORD with all your heart, and do not lean on your own understanding.

Self-Reflection: Scared Texts

1. Which sacred text(s) do you plan on using to help you connect to your higher self during meditations?

   _____
   _____
   _____
   _____
   _____

These are just examples as you may decide to use a different sacred text. The point during meditation is to connect to the Spirit using sacred words to make your connection to the Divine stronger. Now that you have learned the step on how to use a journal to heal your emotional body, it's time to focus on the third step in how to tap into your creative genius.

STEP 3:
Connect With Nature and Its Cousins

It is no surprise that being in nature can give us a sense of our belonging and our connection with everything that exists. I'm not sure if there exists a person who does not feel at peace in nature. This immensely intuitive feeling that nature affords us tranquility and euphoria is theoretically supported by science.

Fundamentally at molecular levels, all living things are of the same physical nature. We are all fundamentally made of variations and assortments of atoms.

At the macro level, nature reminds us of this fact.

To further expound on our molecular connectivity, we are all connected by an invisible web of thought. Our thoughts are made physical by chemicals in our brains which send out physical signals to everything that exists.

This is how bonds are formed between life forms; this is why you and your dog have a mutual connection, or why you feel satisfied upon just seeing your favorite plant. We are all silently communicating with one another and this exemplifies how we are innately all one.

Being reminded of our unity is a special strength we can find through nature. Unity affords us a sense of power; a sense of control. It is comforting and inspiring to be reminded of the fact that we truly are not alone.

In the same way that we have a deep biological love for our parents and vice versa, the biophilia hypothesis makes the claim that humans have an innate tendency to derive euphoria from integrating with nature.

As for our parents, it is in our DNA for them to love us and for us to love them to ensure our survival. As young mammals, our ability to defend ourselves and therefore ensure the survival of our species is limited, therefore we need such a strong bond as love to ensure that it is as hard as possible for our parents to abandon us and easy as possible for them to nurture us.

The same can be said for nature, we experience a deep psychological bond with nature because we need it to survive. In turn, it can be said that nature loves us unconditionally as it is devoted to ensuring that we have all we need to survive. Nature effortlessly and tirelessly supplies us with oxygen, nutrients for energy production, for our diet, water, and raw materials for all the creations we could ever possibly need to make our lives on Earth easier.

Now you can stop wondering why sunsets are so breathtaking, why the sea makes you feel at one with the world and why hiking makes you feel as if you're climbing the staircase to heaven.

Now that we know why we're so inherently pulled toward nature, we can explore the several reasons why connecting to nature is so important.

Keeping Yourself Grounded

Mother Nature is truly our best friend and has several reminders to let us know that. One reason to connect with nature is to keep yourself grounded, especially if you are a highly sensitive spiritual being. You need to connect with nature because your vibration may be very high than your grounding. It is more so important to be grounded so that you can continue to take control of your vibration. For instance, you may be hit with bad news, but instead of going into a depression mode or even becoming more anxious, you are able to stay balanced and think without adding in your emotions. That keeps you in control of the situation and allow you to make decisions better with clarity.

Recognizing You Are a Part of Something Bigger Than Yourself

Being present in nature affords us the opportunity to realize that we are a part of something much larger than ourselves.

When we invest effort to contemplate the stars, the fact that the Universe is a mysterious endless space, the fact that our Earth tirelessly rotates around this omnipresent light source like clockwork, the fact that mountains are just formed and that the waves from the ocean just keep crashing onto the shore like clockwork we realize that there is a much greater force at work in the Universe.

These thoughts allow us to become humble and realize that we are working and living our lives in service to something much greater.

We gain clarity and a rejuvenated view of life which inspires to cast our troubles by the wayside and focus on the bigger picture.

Enjoying the Gift of Being Present

One of the greatest gifts nature has to offer is the opportunity to be truly present. You realize that everything just is. Everything just exists in the present moment with nowhere in particular to go, nothing to do but just exist and keep on existing.

As organisms who have been endowed with an extraordinary level of consciousness, we often misuse our power. Humans suffer from the dreadful affliction of compulsive and unnecessary mental chatter.

This compulsive mental chatter robs us of our time spent living in the present.

We often obsess over future plans, or let our past hold us back. It is rare to find humans truly living in the present moment.

If you've driven from point A to point B without even have the slightest idea of how you got there, then I think you know what I mean.

Due to the breathtaking beauty of nature, when it is truly observed, you lose the ability to compulsively think.

You simply cannot be in the present moment and have excessive mental chatter.

The words 'mind blowing' and 'breath taking', which are often used to describe scenes in nature like the view from a hill top or a sunset, stem from the fact that your mind can't operate compulsively once you are truly engrossed in the present moment. Your mind is blown, it is kaput.

This gift that nature gives, allows us to truly live our lives. The past and future don't exist. Only the present does. Focusing mainly on these compulsive thoughts are a sure way to allow your life to fly past your eyes without you being there.

Spending time in nature and really observing it teaches us the skill of being present.

It is a skill worth cultivating to really be there for one's life. Below are some popular examples of how you can connect with nature:

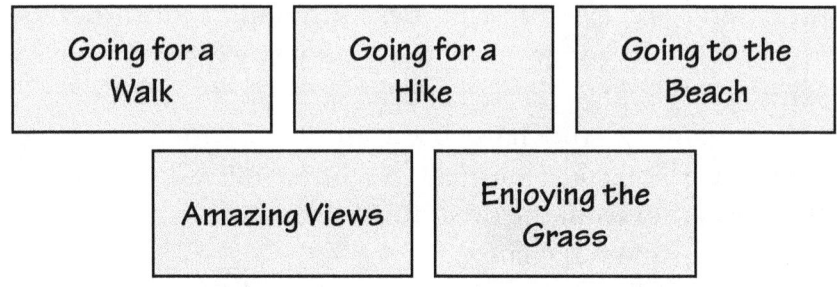

Going For A Walk

Going for a walk, especially in areas with a lot of aspects of nature, like a hiking trail, on a beach or in a forest, allows us to keep moving while fully connecting with nature.

Walking allows us to exercise both our bodies and our minds as we consciously observe the nature around us and feel its energy.

Going To The Beach

It's not a coincidence that almost everyone you know loves going to the beach.

From the soothing sounds of the ocean crashing onto the shore, to the soft relaxing feeling of sand under your toes, going to the beach is one of the most ideal ways to enjoy nature at its finest.

Science suggests that the tranquil blue of the ocean, coupled with the sweet songs of the waves causes a release of endorphins or feel good hormones in our brains. In addition to this, vitamin D, which the sun helps the body to produce, has a profound positive effect on our moods.

Enjoying Grass

Sceneries involving grass can provide tranquility too. Studies have shown that workers who have views of lawns from their offices are less stressed. Viewing or laying in grass is a great way to feel closer to nature. As a suggestion, consider using a blanket or some other covering to lay in the grass, especially if you have any allergies and as a safety precaution. The soothing green and the natural softness of blades of grass are a natural stress reliever. When it comes to connecting with the grass, it allows you to ground yourself as well.

Looking At An Amazing View

Whether you've hiked to the peak of a mountain, drove up to your favorite look out spot or are sitting atop the roof of your house, a killer view makes for a good setting to enjoy the beauty of nature. There's something about overlooking your whole city which makes you feel humble and part of something better. This is a wonderful way to get all the benefits of observing the breathtaking nature, of nature.

If your environment does not have mountains or ocean views, then take in amazing views around your area. For instance, you may see a nice house or even a favorite street sign that brings back fond memories. Whatever strikes your fancy, take a moment and enjoy your environment and let your imagination soar.

Try This...

Take a walk in your neighborhood or just go outside and see if you can find simple reminders and truths that nature wants to share with you.

Self-Reflection: What Did Nature Teach You?

1. What were some reminders and truths that nature shared with you while you were on your walk or just enjoying the outside?

   _____
   _____
   _____
   _____
   _____

2. How did you feel connecting with nature? What was your biggest take-a-way?

   _____
   _____
   _____
   _____
   _____

Getting to Know Nature's Cousins

In addition to integrating with nature, **diet** and **exercise** are key players in the quest for powerful and clear thinking. This is no surprise as you are what you eat. When it comes to trying to access your intuition and creativity, you want to make sure that your messages are clear from the Spirit. Therefore, it is important to try to eat as clean as possible or high-energy foods to help bring mental clarity. After all, the whole point of eating food is to supply your body with nutrients to keep it functioning at its optimal level. Exercise is used to train the body in an effort to keep it optimal.

Self Reflection: What Are You Doing for Exercise?

1. What does your daily exercise routine look like?

   _____
   _____
   _____
   _____
   _____

2. How do you incorporate nature into your exercise routine?

   _____
   _____
   _____
   _____

3. What are some new exercises in which you would like to try?

   _____
   _____
   _____
   _____
   _____

These two elements are therefore essential to the overall functioning of the body, therefore they are instrumental in promoting clear and powerful brain function.

A plant based diet especially has a profound impact on mental functions as it eradicates dangerous processed foods from the diet. Studies have shown that plant based diets reduce the amount of inflammation occurring in the body and antioxidants present in plant based products repair damaged cells more quickly and efficiently.

Self Reflection: What Are You Putting in Your Body?

1. What does your diet look like? Is it plant-based? Why or why not?

   _____
   _____
   _____
   _____
   _____

2. How do you incorporate meal-planning into your diet?

   _____
   _____
   _____
   _____
   _____

3. What are some new recipes in which you would like to try?

   _____
   _____
   _____
   _____
   _____

In addition to this, they have a uniquely distinct function in the brain where they promote a healthy balance of necessary neurotransmitters. Exercise has a similar effect.

To get the most out of a healthy diet, meal planning is of utmost importance.

Helpful Tips for Planning Meals

1. Invest time in researching recipes
2. Invest time in grocery shopping garnering all you will need for each recipe
3. Plan for at least an entire week's worth of meals to enhance consistency
4. Dedicate a specific space to record meal plans
5. Document your progress
6. Hold yourself accountable
7. Snack healthily in between big meals to prevent straying from the diet
8. Freeze as much as possible
9. Find online recipes with shared ingredients

It can be a bit of a challenge to stick to a regimen without falling off the wagon, so to speak. Therefore, do not judge yourself if you encounter resistance to sticking to the schedule. This is normal when trying to implement change.

It's important to be gentle with yourself. Please do keep in mind that resistance is normal, and it takes a while for a habit to change; science says around 30 days to be exact. The more you focus on the times that you do get it right, the more you will get it right.

In this step, you learned that nature is truly your best friend because it helps you bring clarity. In other words, while being in nature we start to see things not as they appear to be, but as they are. We can use this newfound clarity to carefully think and act on our own lives. By connecting with nature, it will enhance your chances of connecting to your intuition and a sense of peace knowing that you are one with the Universe.

STEP 4:
Sustaining A Meditation Practice

Would you consider yourself a "veteran meditator?" Are you new to the practice? Maybe you don't have any experience whatsoever with meditation. Perhaps you are skeptical of the practice of meditation altogether. Regardless of your level of expertise, there is always room to grow and develop as a meditator. Whether you are looking to enhance your practice, searching for ways to sustain your practice, or are wondering which type of meditation practice is a good fit for you, there are countless ways to deepen and improve your meditation experience.

Why Meditate?

No matter how long you have or have not been meditating, it's important to have a strong awareness as to why meditation is such a powerful practice to incorporate into your daily life. If you don't know why you want to meditate, you are unlikely to receive any benefit from it in the first place. If you allow it, meditation has the power to transform your mind, body, and spirit in ways you could have never imagined. Some of the most basic benefits of meditation are a greater sense of calm, increased focus and attention, and a greater connection to your surroundings. According to Sharon Salzberg, cofounder of the Insight Meditation Society, offers additional meditation benefits such as: you will have better coping mechanisms for dealing with pain and difficult emotions, you'll have a deeper sense of self, and you'll have a renewed sense of energy. Moreover, the combination of each of these benefits together simply creates for a happier you.

Conflicts with Meditation

You may be asking yourself, if the benefits of meditation are so strong, why doesn't every single person in the world meditate on a daily basis? Aside from the religious stigma that is still tied to meditation, it's not as easy as it sounds to build and sustain a consistent meditation practice. Whether you are a veteran meditator or just starting out, you know how easy it is to get carried away by your own thoughts. As hard as you try to focus on your breath, you realize that your thoughts have a mind of their own. This can be quite frustrating, enough so that beginning meditators may abandon the practice before really giving it a fair chance. If you are able to ride this initial wave of frustration, you may then encounter the difficulties of sustaining a daily practice. With families, children, work, and countless other responsibilities, it can be incredibly hard to simply find the time to meditate. It can feel like one more thing on your "to do" list that you need to cross off, rather than an opportunity for self-exploration and growth. It is much easier to abandon the practice altogether, than it is to build an ongoing habit that becomes a part of your daily life. However, if you are committed to building a strong, consistent, and positive meditation practice, there are some strategies and tools that can help you overcome these conflicts.

Sustaining Your Meditation Practice

First and foremost, it's important to know that no two meditation sessions will be the same. Like snowflakes, each meditation will look and feel different. This doesn't mean you are having a "good" or "bad" meditation session. Before you can allow yourself to sustain a meditation practice, you must release all judgement of yourself as a meditator. Once you let go of this expectation of having "good" and transformative meditations every time you sit, you are more likely to keep up with the practice on a daily basis.

Start Small

When you are first starting out, start small. Make a commitment to yourself to meditate at least 10 minutes a day for a month. While you will find much more benefit from longer meditations, it is more important to build up your stamina by starting with smaller increments. If you find that even 10 minutes is too much to start, allow yourself to commit to 5 minutes or even 1 minute. When it feels comfortable to you, increase your meditation periods by 5 or 10 minutes. If you are in it for the "long haul", it's more important to get into the habit of meditating on a daily basis than it is to meditate for 30 minutes once a week.

Find A Meditation Buddy

You've heard of people having a "work out buddy." Well, that can apply to meditation as well! Find a friend who is just as motivated to sustain a meditation practice as you are. This friend should encourage you to meditate every day. It could be something as simple as a text message that says: "Have you meditated yet today?" Perhaps you might even find a time and place to meditate together. With a meditation buddy, you are just as responsible for reminding your friend to meditate as your friend is responsible for reminding you. This responsibility alone will help keep you committed to your practice. Not only are you accountable for yourself, but you are accountable for someone else as well.

Build Meditation Into Your Daily Schedule

You likely have a routine that you follow to get you through your day. For example, you might wake up, shower, get dressed, eat breakfast, go to work, come home, make dinner, do your chores, etc. One of the best ways to ensure that meditation becomes a part of your daily life is to treat it as important as showering or making dinner. Decide where meditation best fits into your day. Does it feel right to meditate when you are still lying in bed, first thing in the morning? Would it feel better to meditate for 5 minutes while sitting in your car, before heading into work? Be creative and open minded. Meditation can happen anywhere, anytime, as long as you are free of noise and distractions.

Track Your Meditation Activities

An additional way to stay committed to your practice is to track your meditation activities. This could be something as simple as a chart where you write the total number of minutes you meditate each day. At the end of the week, you add up the total minutes you have meditated. With this system, you can analyze which days of the week you meditate longer, which weeks you meditate for more minutes altogether, and how you compare from month to month. It could also be something as simple as creating a chart where you simply color in a box each day you meditate. Along the same lines, you can determine which days you are more likely to meditate. At the same time, you encourage yourself to meditate each day so that you don't have any boxes uncolored. Cory Muscara, founder of the Long Island Center for Mindfulness, has created a Meditation Chain Method for the purpose of tracking your meditation sessions.

A sample of this Meditation Chain Method can be seen below:

Dates	
Dates	
Dates	
Dates	

Credit: Cory Muscara. Meditation Chain Method

There's An App For That

Several apps have also been developed to help people sustain and track their meditation activities. Many apps offer guided meditations, visualizations, timers, and tips for meditating. One of the best apps for sustaining a meditation practice is the *Insight Timer* app. This app offers thousands of meditations in addition to a simple bell, helping to start and end each meditation session. Moreover, the app tracks your consecutive days of practice, the number of minutes spent in guided meditation, and the number of minutes spent in timed meditation. A bar graph tracks your progress over time, allowing a visual representation of when and how often you meditate. Moreover, the app offers "milestones" for various consecutive days of meditation as well as total days of meditation. These milestones are symbolized with a colored star next to your name. The more colored stars you have, the more milestones you have reached. This simple tool is a powerful motivator to continue meditating on a day-to-day basis.

Set Yourself Free

Now that you have a basic understanding of the power of meditation and some tips for sustaining a meditation practice over an extended time period, it is time to set yourself free. Open yourself to the miracle of meditation and all the beautiful transformations that are out in the universe, waiting just for you. Remember not to be too hard on yourself and not to judge your practice. Keep an open mind and be patient. Change doesn't happen overnight, nor does a consistent meditation practice. Lastly, remember that meditation is just that: a practice. The more you meditate, the more benefits you will see, the more transformations you will experience, and the happier you will become. Let's look at the fifth step on how to tap into your creative genius.

STEP 5: Practice Mindfulness and Track It

Where are you right now? Sure, you might say you are sitting down, reading this book. What a silly question, right? But, I beg you to think about this question a little deeper: Where are you *really* right now? Think about it. Are you attending to the words on the page, but actually creating a to-do list in your mind of all the things you need to accomplish when you get home? Do the laundry, wash the dishes, take out the garbage, make dinner, RSVP to that dinner party, pay the cable bill. Maybe you're recalling the events of your day as you are reading the words on this page; perhaps, you are still sitting in that long meeting, frustrated that someone could waste your time when you could be doing a million other, more productive tasks. As great as your intentions are to sit and simply focus on reading this book, chances are, you're in many more places and thoughts than you realize. In Step 4, you learned about meditation. It's important to understand that mindfulness is a part of meditation because meditation is a way to gain access to your intuition. In fact, mindfulness is a type of meditation that focuses on the act of focusing on being in the present. On that note, let's take a closer look at mindfulness and how to track it.

Mindfulness 101

According to Jon Kabat-Zinn, creator of the Stress Reduction Clinic and the Center for Mindfulness in Medicine, Healthcare, and Society at the University of Massachusetts Medical School, Mindfulness is "paying attention, on purpose, in the present moment, nonjudgmentally, for the cultivation of wisdom and compassion." In other words, Mindfulness is the practice of focusing on the here and the now: the past is over and the future isn't here yet. To do so nonjudgmentally is not to label your thoughts or feelings as good or bad, but to simply observe them from a distance. Over time, you'll develop a greater sense of compassion toward all beings, including yourself, and you'll come to possess a unique wisdom about the world around you. Of course, the practice of Mindfulness yields countless additional benefits such as helping you to create and maintain healthier, more balanced relationships, an increase in focus and attention, a greater sense of patience, greater control over strong emotions (both good and bad), and above all, you will become a happier, more satisfied human being.

Now what?

You may be thinking to yourself, "Yeah, Mindfulness sounds great, but now what?" How can you get yourself from a place of emotionally charged chaos to one of peace and serenity? Where do you begin? There are opportunities in every single moment of every single day for you to practice Mindfulness. In the beginning, it's hard to see these moments because our thoughts and feelings are so caught up in running on autopilot. Therefore, it's important to dedicate time to a few specific exercises and techniques that will helps to create the necessary foundation for cultivating a more mindful lifestyle. When you are first starting to practice Mindfulness, it is beneficial to keep track of the activities you are doing. This will help to keep you more accountable for devoting the time to Mindfulness, which will eventually just become a part of your everyday life.

Mindful Mornings

There is no better way to start your day than with Mindfulness. This can be accomplished in a couple of different ways. Before jumping out of bed to start your day, take a moment to set an intention for the day. What do you want to be your goal or focus for the day? Reflect on what kind of day you would like to have. For example, you might set an intention along the lines of: "Today, I will be patient and productive." Keep your intention simple so that you are more inclined to accomplish it. Once your intention is set, just take a few deep breaths before heading on to the next part of your morning. If you have the time, you might even want to do a brief meditation. All of this helps to calm your mind and get you grounded for the day ahead.

As you get out of bed, play some calming music in the background if it is possible. In the moments of silence, you will be carried away by the serenity in the music. The music may even encourage silence for you and your other family members may just want to focus on the music in the background. Moreover, the presence of the calming music may be a reminder to you to focus on being more mindful. You can be mindful while brushing your teeth, eating your breakfast, and even while getting dressed. In each of these moments, don't let your mind get carried away by the stories of your thoughts. Rather, focus on the sensations of the senses in each moment. For example, when brushing your teeth, you might focus on the smell of the toothpaste, the feel of the bristles against your teeth and tongue, the feel of the toothpaste foaming inside your mouth, the sound of the bristles against your teeth, and so on.

At this point in time, you may be feeling overwhelmed with all of the opportunities for Mindfulness that are available to you in your mornings. You may be thinking to yourself: "Well, this all sounds great and everything, but I really don't have the time to think about what my clothes feel like against my skin as I'm getting dressed in the morning." Therefore, it's important to start small. Attached is a chart that can help you narrow down your focus of morning Mindfulness activities without feeling overwhelmed. Perhaps, you just want to include 1-2 activities in your morning. As these activities become a part of your daily routine, you can consider additional activities. It might be helpful to place this chart in a highly visible area such as the refrigerator or on the bathroom door. After you accomplish an activity, just put a check next to it. This will help you to keep track of the activities you are completing each day. You'll become aware of the activities you are more likely to accomplish and which ones you find most beneficial in your morning. There's also a space for you to write in any comments about the activity that you might want to remember for the future. It could be something as simple as "easy to do" or "felt really good." As you become more comfortable with your Mindful practice in the mornings, you can modify the chart so that it fits your individual needs.

Mindful Afternoons/Evenings

Similar to the morning, there are numerous opportunities to incorporate Mindfulness activities throughout the rest of your day. It may seem impossible to consider being mindful at work, but believe it or not, it is possible! You'll notice that the attached chart also includes options for your workday and your evening. Again, this is just a small sample of the activities that can be easily integrated into your day. Depending on the kind of work you do, you may want to alter the chart accordingly. Think about the times throughout your work day where you might be able to be just a little bit more mindful. The more mindful you become, the more opportunities that you'll see in your day-to-day life.

Mindfulness Now

You don't have to wait until tomorrow morning to begin your Mindfulness journey. What better time to begin than this present moment? Any moment can be transformed into a mindful moment by asking yourself the following questions: What is happening right now? What am I doing right now? How does it feel? How do I feel? What sensations can I feel throughout my body? How is my breathing? What can I hear/smell right now? By asking yourself these questions, you are forcing yourself to observe the present moment as it is happening right now. It helps slow down the autopilot mode, even for just a brief minute or two. It won't be long before you'll realize that these thoughts become a part of your regular, everyday thoughts. You will notice yourself becoming more mindful spontaneously without having to try so purposely. You'll catch yourself being kinder to yourself, more compassionate towards others, more patient, in more control of your emotions, and simply more aware of your surroundings. The sunrises will be more beautiful, birds chirping will sound like natural music, your skin will tingle as the wind brushes against you. You will observe more miracles in your day-to-day life than you ever thought possible. Above all, you will be happy. Now, that you have learned about meditation and mindfulness, it's time to take your spiritual practice to the next level by connecting with your Angels.

STEP 6:
Get to Know Your Angels By Name

Now, we are focusing on the last step on how to tap into your creative genius. A lot of people are not well-verse in all of the Archangels, but there are more than the few that are mentioned in Theology. There are hundreds, perhaps thousands, of archangels in the Universe. You will know when you come into contact with them because the vast majority of these angels and archangels are helpful, loving, trustworthy, and known for doing good in this world. However, you must test every spirit in which you decide to make a connection with.

I want to highlight and focus on the 15 Archangels that we work with in our healing center. It really depends on the situation and what the Spirit shares with us and who is assigned to help us heal our clients.

When I attended the Southwest Institute of Healing Arts, I took a course on Archangels and studied Doreen Virtue's work. While we have a plethora of true events that clients have shared with us or we have bear witness to of how Angels communicate with us in the modern world, we wanted to make sure that we provide proper attribute of where we got our information on Archangels since Dr. Doreen Virtue is one of the leading spiritual authorities on this topic.

The following excerpt is taken from the book ARCHANGELS 101: How to Connect Closely with Archangels Michael, Raphael, Gabriel, Uriel, and Others for Healing, Protection, and Guidance by Doreen Virtue.

It is published by Hay House (October 2010) and is available at all bookstores or online at: www.hayhouse.com.

Who Are the Archangels?

The word archangel is derived from the Greek archi, which means "first, principal, or chief"; and angelos, which means "messenger of God." So, archangels are the chief messengers of God.

Archangels are extremely powerful celestial beings. Each has a specialty and represents an aspect of God. You can think of archangels as facets on the face of God, the ultimate jewel and gem of the universe. These facets, or archangels, are prisms that radiate Divine light and love in specific ways to everyone on Earth.

The archangels are one of God's original creations, and they existed long before humankind or organized religions. They belong to God, not to any specific theology. Therefore, archangels work with people of all different beliefs and paths. In fact, they work with anyone who asks.

Artwork portrays archangels as ideal human forms with large eagle- or swanlike wings, in contrast to artistic depictions of cherubs as babies with small wings.

Below are the list of Archangels and what they specialize in to assist you on your own life journey:

Archangels By Name	When to Call Upon These Archangels
Ariel (Prosperity)	Helps with your material needs being provided as you follow your intuition and manifest your dreams into reality.
Azrael (Comfort)	Helps with all aspects of loss, death, and transitions.
Chamuel (Peace)	Helps you find what you're looking for and helps bring inner peace.
Gabriel (Creative Writing)	Make time to write down your thoughts in a journal, or pen an article or book.
Haniel (Sensitivity)	Helps you develop your intuition and clairvoyance, as well as, any aspect of sacred feminine energy.
Jeremiel (All is Well)	Helps develop an understanding of spiritual visions and clairvoyance. Helps you conduct a life review so you can make adjustments with respect to how you want to live your life in the present and future.
Jophiel (Outdoors)	Helps you quickly shift from a negative to a positive mindset. Helps you reduce clutter in the home and office.
Metatron (Prioritize)	Focus on your highest priorities. I will help you get organized and motivated.

Michael (Crystal-Clear Intentions)	Be clear about what you desire and focus upon it with unwavering faith.
Raguel (Divine Order)	Known for healing arguments or misunderstandings. He brings forgiveness, peace, calm; attracts wonderful friends who treat you with respect and integrity.
Raphael (Angel Therapy)	Wants us to give your cares and worries to us angels, and allow us to take your burdens.
Raziel (Take Your Power Back)	Helps you recall lessons that your soul has accumulated over time. Helps heal painful memories, past traumas, and fears to move forward in life.
Sandalphon (Gifts from God)	Helps being an intercessor for prayers between humans and God; helping determine the gender of a coming child, and helps musicians.
Uriel (Claircognizance)	Illuminates our mind with information, ideas, epiphanies, and insights. He whispers correct and appropriate answers as you will receive words, thoughts, and visions suddenly downloaded into your mind.
Zadkiel (Clairaudience)	Helps students remember facts and figures for tests; healing painful memories; remembering your Divine spiritual origin and missions, and choosing forgiveness.

The Nine Choirs of Angels

Angelology, the study of angels, holds that there are nine "choirs" or branches of angels, which include:

1. **Seraphim:** These are the highest order of angels, said to be shining bright, as they are closest to God. They are pure light.
2. **Cherubim:** Usually portrayed as chubby children with wings à la Cupid, the Cherubim are the second-highest order. They are pure love.
3. **Thrones:** The triad of Seraphim, Cherubim, and Thrones resides in the highest realms of Heaven. Thrones are the bridge between the material and the spiritual, and represent God's fairness and justice.
4. **Dominions:** The Dominions are the highest in the next triad level of angels. They are the overseers or managers of angels, according to God's will.
5. **Virtues:** These angels govern the order of the physical universe, watching over the sun, moon, stars, and all of the planets, including Earth.
6. **Powers:** As their name implies, this choir comprises peaceful warriors who purify the universe from lower energies.
7. **Principalities:** The third triad are the angels closest to Earth. The Principalities watch over the planet, including nations and cities, to ensure God's will of peace on Earth.
8. **Archangels:** These are the overseers of humankind and the guardian angels. Each archangel has a speciality representing an aspect of God.
9. **Guardian angels:** You, and every individual, have personal guardian angels assigned to you throughout your life.

This model of nine choirs was derived from the biblical references to Seraphim and Cherubim, which were expanded upon in the 5th-century theologian Pseudo-Dionysius's writings and then popularized in John Milton's poetic work *Paradise Lost*.

Interacting with Archangels

Since archangels are so close to Earth and humankind, it's natural for us to connect with them. In fact, the Bible is filled with accounts of people interacting with Michael and Gabriel. The archangels still interact with us in conjunction with God's will of peace.

We don't pray to archangels, nor do we worship them. All glory goes to God. We work with archangels simply because they are God's intended gift to us all, and part of the divine plan for peace.

So why don't we simply direct all questions and requests to God? Because the archangels are extensions of God who are easier to hear and feel during times of great stress. Their vibrations are very condensed, and they're palpable and practically tangible. Just as looking at a sunset or a rainbow reminds us of God's love, so do the archangels.

You don't need to be saintly or a perfectly behaved person to elicit the archangels' help. They look past human mistakes and see the inner goodness within us all. They want to bring peace to Earth by helping us all be *peaceful*. So their mission includes helping the *un*peaceful people of the world.

As holograms of God's omnipresence, the archangels are unlimited beings. Remember the promise that Jesus made: "I am with you always"? Well, the archangels—like Jesus—are able to be with each person who calls upon them.

The key is that the archangels will never violate your free will by intervening without permission, even if to do so would make us happier. They must wait until you give permission in some way: a prayer, a cry for help, a wish, a visualization, an affirmation, or a thought. The archangels don't care *how* you ask for their help, but only that you *do*.

You also needn't worry about asking for the archangels' help incorrectly. You don't have to be specially trained or use fancy invocations to garner their attention. Any sincere call for aid is enough, as all they require is your permission.

Affirmative and supplicant prayers work. In the former, it's a positive here-and-now statement or visualization, such as "Thank you, Archangel Michael, for protecting me"; and in the latter, it's an appeal, like "Please protect, Archangel Michael." Both yield the same results.

This is also the answer when asking, "Should I call upon God directly? Should I ask God to send the appropriate angels? Or should I call the angels

directly?" These questions imply that there's a separation between God and the angels, and there is not.

Message from Minister Alise

So, as you can see, the Archangels are extremely important to us. For further reading, please do check out Doreen Virtue's work on Angels and Angel Therapy. We are a huge fan of her and Dr. Virtue's work helped me better understand myself, since I am an Earth Angel and am here to serve humanity with love and light.

What are Angel Numbers?

One of the most common ways in which angels speak to you is by showing you repetitive number sequences. If you see a repetitive number sequence over and over again, your Angels are trying to tell you something. It is important to interpret these messages from your guardians so that you can know what the warning, message, or insight is coming in for you. Doreen Virtue's best-selling book, Angel Numbers 101: The meaning of 111, 123, 444 and Other Number Sequences is a great way to help you with that. You may also visit her website at the following: https://www.angeltherapy.com/angel-numbers

We are still gathering client stories of how Angels have communicated to them using these Angel Numbers and will share them with you at a later time.

If you have a story that you would like to share with us, please email them to support@alisehealingcenter.com with Angel Numbers Encounter Story in the Subject Line.

You have learned all of the steps on how to tap into your creative genius. As you continue to connect with your intuition and Angels, you will discover that they will help you advance your spiritual practice so that you can continue to live life boldly and intuitively.

Where To Go From Here

You can check out the Alise Spiritual Healing & Wellness Center to see how to schedule a creative strategy session, intuitive reading, life coaching session, flower essence session, or just to hang out and learn what we are all about. Our website is the following: www.alisehealingcenter.com.

Looking for a guest speaker? Please go to our website and invite Alise to speak.

Should you have questions or comments for us, suggestions for future material or tips, feel free to email us at support@alisehealingcenter.com

Class Tours and Conferences

Please check our website on upcoming events at www.alisehealingcenter.com.

Also, we have an annual Women's Love of You Conference and you can check upcoming events at www.love-ofyouconference.com.

You can also join our mailing list or email us at support@alisehealingcenter.com.

NOTES

NOTES

NOTES

NOTES

NOTES

NOTES

NOTES

NOTES

NOTES